VOL. II Great Popular MUSIC

Easy Piano Arrangements by DAN COATES

MW01109437

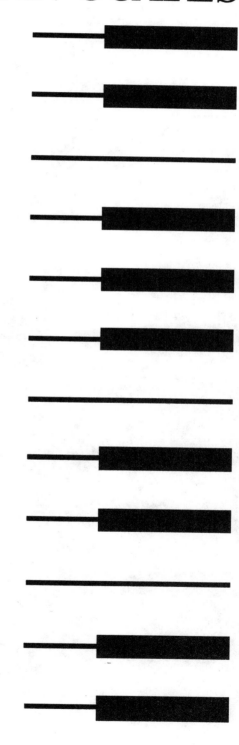

Project Manager: Carol Cuellar • Book Layout: Debbie Lipton • Cover Image © J-P Nova, PicturePerfect USA, Inc.
© 1996 WARNER BROS. PUBLICATIONS INC. • All Rights Reserved

Any duplication, adaptation or arrangement of the compositions contained in this collection requires the written consent of the Publisher. No part of this book may be photocopied or reduced in any way without permission. Unauthorized uses are an infringement of U.S. Copyright Act and are punishable by law.

Foreword

Dan Coates

One of today's foremost personalities in the field of printed music, Dan Coates has been providing teachers and professional musicians with quality piano material since 1975. Equally adept in arranging for beginners or accomplished musicians, his Big Note, Easy Piano and Professional Touch arrangements have made a significant contribution to the industry.

Born in Syracuse, New York, Dan began to play piano at age four. By the time he was 15, he'd won a New York State competition for music composers. After high school graduation, he toured the United States, Canada and Europe as an arranger and pianist with the world-famous group "Up With People".

Dan settled in Miami, Florida, where he studied piano with Ivan Davis at the University of Miami while playing professionally throughout southern Florida. To date, his performance credits include appearances on "Murphy Brown," "My Sister Sam" and at the Opening Ceremonies of the 1984 Summer Olympics in Los Angeles. Dan has also accompanied such artists as Dusty Springfield and Charlotte Rae.

In 1982, Dan began his association with Warner Bros. Publications - an association which has produced more than 400 Dan Coates books and sheets. Throughout the year he conducts piano workshops nation-wide, during which he demonstrates his popular arrangements.

Contents

TEARS IN HEAVEN

Words and Music by
WILL JENNINGS and ERIC CLAPTON
Arranged by DAN COATES

Tears in Heaven - 4 - 1

Copyright © 1992 BLUE SKY RIDER SONGS (BMI) & DRUMLIN' LTD. (PRS)
All Rights Administered by RONDOR MUSIC (LONDON) LTD. (PRS) on behalf of the BLUE SKY RIDER SONGS/
IRVING MUSIC, INC. (BMI) Administers in the U.S. and Canada
International Copyright Secured   Made in U.S.A.   All Rights Reserved

6

ANGEL EYES

Composed by
JIM BRICKMAN
Arranged by DAN COATES

Angel Eyes - 3 - 1

© 1995 BRICKMAN ARRANGEMENT (SESAC) & SWIMMER MUSIC (SESAC)
All Rights Reserved

10

Angel Eyes - 3 - 3

BECAUSE YOU LOVED ME
(Theme from "Up Close & Personal")

Words and Music by
DIANE WARREN
Arrnaged by DAN COATES

Because You Loved Me - 5 - 1

© 1996 REALSONGS (ASCAP)
All Rights Reserved

12

be - for - ev - er thank - ful, ba - by. You're the one ___ who held ___
grate - ful for ___ each day ___ you gave me. May - be I ___ don't know ___

___ me up, ___ nev - er let ___ me fall.
___ that much, ___ but I know this much ___ is true:

You're the one ___ who saw ___ me through, through it all. ___
I was blessed be - cause ___ I was loved by you. ___

You were ___ my strength when I ___ was weak, you were ___ my

Because You Loved Me - 5 - 2

14

15

Because You Loved Me - 5 - 5

BLUE

Words and Music by
BILL MACK
Arranged by DAN COATES

Blue, oh, so lone-some for you. Why can't you be blue o-ver me? Blue, oh, so

Blue - 3 - 1

© 1966 (Renewed 1994) TRIO MUSIC CO., INC. and FORT KNOX MUSIC, INC.
This Arrangement © 1996 TRIO MUSIC CO., INC. and FORT KNOX MUSIC, INC.
All Rights Reserved

Verse 2:
Now that it's over,
I realize
Those sweet words you whispered
Were nothing but lies.
(To Chorus:)

I DO

Words and Music by
PAUL BRANDT
Arranged by DAN COATES

© 1996 WARNER-TAMERLANE PUBLISHING CORP. and POLLYWOG MUSIC
All Rights Administered by WARNER-TAMERLANE PUBLISHING CORP.
All Rights Reserved

20

I Do - 3 - 2

Verse 3:
I know the time will disappear,
But this love we're building on will always be here.
No way that this is sinking sand,
On this solid rock we'll stand forever.
(To Chorus:)

CANON IN D
(Pachelbel)

By
JOHANN PACHELBEL
Arranged by DAN COATES

© 1996 WB MUSIC CORP.
All Rights Reserved

Canon in D - 4 - 4

CHANGE THE WORLD

Words and Music by
TOMMY SIMS, GORDON KENNEDY
and WAYNE KIRKPATRICK
Arranged by DAN COATES

Change the World - 4 - 1

© 1996 WB MUSIC CORP., INTERSCOPE MUSIC PUBLISHING, INC., BASES LOADED MUSIC,
YELLOW JACKET MUSIC, POLYGRAM INTERNATIONAL PUBLISHING, INC., MAGIC BEANS MUSIC and EMILY BOOTHE, INC.
All Rights on behalf of INTERSCOPE MUSIC PUBLISHING, INC. Administered by WB MUSIC CORP.
All Rights Reserved

28

Change the World - 4 - 3

DREAMING OF YOU

Words and Music by
TOM SNOW and
FRAN GOLDE
Arranged by DAN COATES

Dreaming of You - 4 - 1

© 1989, 1995 SNOW MUSIC (ASCAP)/VIRGIN MUSIC, INC./CHESCA TUNES (BMI)
All Rights Reserved

I'LL BE THERE FOR YOU
(Theme from "Friends")

Words by
DAVID CRANE, MARTA KAUFFMAN, ALLEE WILLIS,
PHIL SOLEM and DANNY WILDE

Music by
MICHAEL SKLOFF
Arranged by DAN COATES

I'll Be There for You - 6 - 1

© 1994 WB MUSIC CORP. and WARNER-TAMERLANE PUBLISHING CORP.
This Arrangement © 1995 WB MUSIC CORP. and WARNER-TAMERLANE PUBLISHING CORP.
All Rights Reserved

38

KILLING ME SOFTLY
(With His Song)

Words by
NORMAN GIMBEL

Music by
CHARLES FOX
Arranged by DAN COATES

Moderately slow

Strum - ming my pain ___ with his fin - gers, ___ sing - ing my life ___ with his words.

Kill - ing me soft - ly with his ___ song, kill - ing me soft -

ly with his ___ song. Tell - ing my whole ___ life with his ___

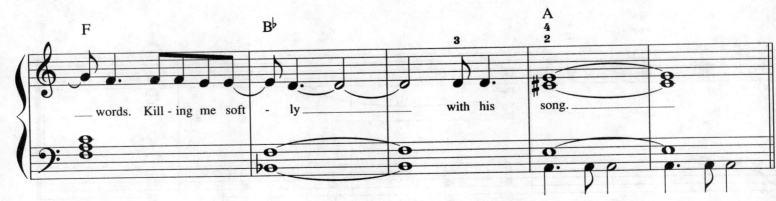

words. Kill - ing me soft - ly ___ with his song. ___

© 1972 CHARLES FOX and NORMAN GIMBEL
This Arrangement © 1996 CHARLES FOX and NORMAN GIMBEL
FOX-GIMBLE PRODUCTIONS, INC., Box 1138, Beverly Hills, CA. 90213
All Rights Reserved

Killing Me Softly - 3 - 2

Verse 3:
He sang as if he knew me,
In all my dark despair.
And then he looked right through me
As if I wasn't there.
But he was there, this stranger
Singing clear and strong. *(To Chorus:)*

LANE'S THEME

Composed by
BILL CONTI
Arranged by DAN COATES

Slowly, with expression ♩ = 60

Lane's Theme - 3 - 1
International Copyright Secured   Copyright © 1994 BILL CONTI   All Rights Reserved
Made in U.S.A.

44

Lane's Theme - 3 - 2

LIKE THE RAIN

Words and Music by
CLINT BLACK and HAYDEN NICHOLAS
Arranged by DAN COATES

Moderately slow

never liked the rain _____ 'til I walked through it with you. _____ Ev - 'ry

thun - der cloud that came _ was one more I might not get through. _ But on the

dark - est day there's al - ways light, and now I see it, too. _ But I

Like the Rain - 5 - 1

© 1994 BLACKENED MUSIC
All Rights Reserved

48

rain.

rain. I have fall-en for you, I'm fall-ing for you now, just like __ the rain. And when the

night falls on our bet-ter days __ and we're look-in' to the sky __ for the

Like the Rain - 5 - 3

50

Verse 2:
I hear it falling in the night and filling up my mind.
All the heavens' rivers come to light and I see it all unwind.
I hear it talking through the trees and on the window pane,
And when I hear it, I just can't believe I never liked the rain.
Like the rain...   *(To Chorus:)*

Verse 3:
When the cloud is rolling over, thunder striking me,
It's as bright as lightning and I wonder why I couldn't see
That it's always good and when the flood is gone we still remain.
Guess I've known all along I just belong here with you falling
Like the rain...   *(To Chorus:)*

MORE THAN WORDS

Lyrics and Music by
BETTENCOURT, CHERONE
Arranged by DAN COATES

More Than Words - 5 - 1

© 1990 FUNKY METAL PUBLISHING (ASCAP)
All Rights Administered by ALMO MUSIC CORP. (ASCAP)
International Copyright Secured   Made in U.S.A.   All Rights Reserved

54

Verse 2:
Now that I have tried to talk to you
And make you understand,
All you have to do is close your eyes
And just reach out your hands
And touch me, hold me close, don't ever let me go.
More than words is all I ever needed you to show.
Then you wouldn't have to say
That you love me, 'cause I'd already know.

LINUS AND LUCY

By VINCE GUARALDI
Arranged by DAN COATES

Linus and Lucy - 2 - 1

© LEE MENDELSON FILM PRODUCTIONS, INC., 1965 (Renewed)
All Rights Reserved

ONE CLEAR VOICE

Words and Music by
J.D. MARTIN and MARC BEESON
Arranged by DAN COATES

© 1995, 1996 WB MUSIC CORP., MIGHT BE MUSIC,
EMI APRIL MUSIC INC. and K-TOWN MUSIC (ASCAP)
All Rights on behalf of MIGHT BE MUSIC Administered by WB MUSIC CORP.
All Rights Reserved

60

REACH

Words and Music by
GLORIA ESTEFAN and
DIANE WARREN
Arranged by DAN COATES

1. Some dreams live on in time for - ev - er.
2. Some days are meant to be re - mem - bered.

Those dreams you want with all your heart.
Those days, we rise a - bove the stars.

And I'll
So, I'll

Reach - 5 - 1

© 1995, 1996 FOREIGN IMPORTED PRODUCTIONS & PUBLISHING, INC. (BMI) / REALSONGS (ASCAP)
All Rights Reserved

62

do / go — what - ev - er it / the dis - tance this — takes, / time, — fol - low through / see - ing more

— / — with / the — the prom - ise I / high - er I — made, / climb — put it / that the

all / more on I the be line, — / lieve, — what I / all the hope for / more that at last — / this dream — would be / will be mine } / mine } — if I could

reach — high - er, — just for one

Reach - 5 - 5

Theme Song from the Mirisch-G&E Production, "THE PINK PANTHER," a United Artists Release

THE PINK PANTHER

Music by
HENRY MANCINI
Arranged by DAN COATES

The Pink Panther - 2 - 1

© 1963 (Renewed 1991) NORTHRIDGE MUSIC COMPANY and EMI U CATALOG INC.
Print Rights on behalf of EMI U CATALOG INC. Administered by WARNER BROS. PUBLICATIONS U.S. INC.
All Rights Reserved

The Pink Panther - 2 - 2

SEND IN THE CLOWNS
(From "A Little Night Music")

Music and Lyrics by
STEPHEN SONDHEIM
Arranged by DAN COATES

Slowly, with expression

© 1973 RILTING MUSIC, INC. (ASCAP)
All Rights Reserved   Used by Permission

70

Send in the Clowns - 4 - 3

STAIRWAY TO HEAVEN

Words and Music by
JIMMY PAGE and ROBERT PLANT
Arranged by DAN COATES

© 1972, 1983 SUPERHYPE PUBLISHING
All rights administered by WB MUSIC CORP.
All Rights Reserved

74

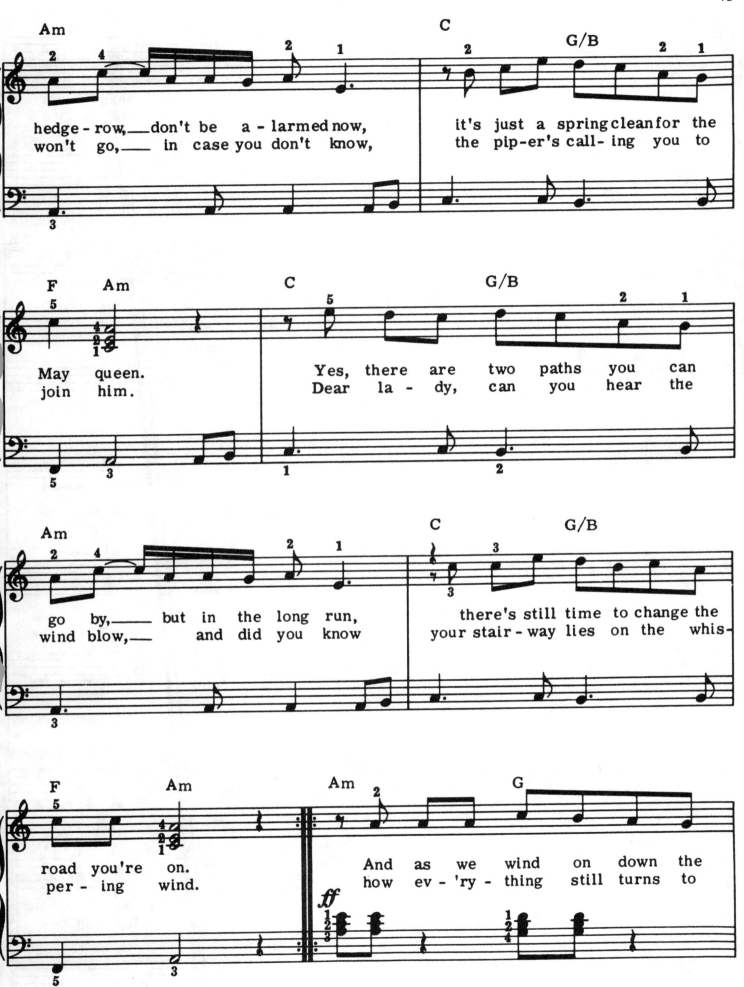

From the Motion Picture "ANNIE"

TOMORROW

Lyrics by
MARTIN CHARNIN

Music by
CHARLES STROUSE
Arranged by DAN COATES

Tomorrow - 3 - 1

© 1977 CHARLES STROUSE and EDWIN H. MORRIS & CO.
Rights for CHARLES STROUSE Administered by MUSIQUE ENTERPRISES INTERNATIONAL, INC.
All Rights Reserved

79

Tomorrow - 3 - 3